CROSS

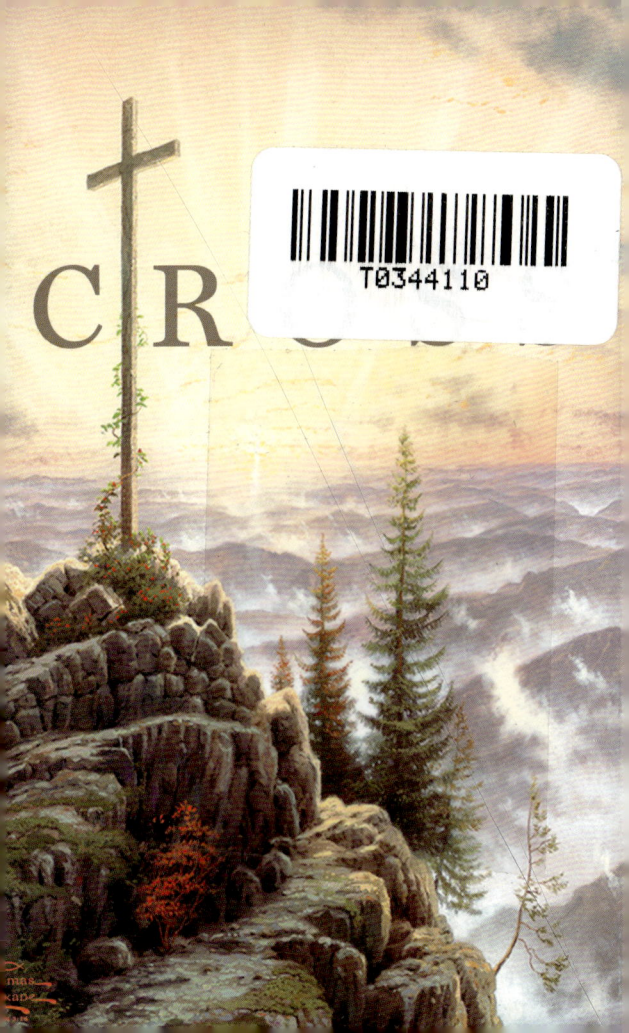

There have been few methods of execution more excruciatingly painful than crucifixion, and the Romans mastered it.

By design, death on a cross was not quick. Soldiers would first whip the victim with a scourge and then force him to carry his own crossbeam to the execution site. Once suspended on a cross, the hours in a strained position took a toll, causing difficulty in breathing and often resulting in suffocation. Some victims would hang alive for days, finally succumbing to death as a welcome relief.

It wasn't until AD 337 that crucifixion was banned in Rome by the first Christian emperor, Constantine the Great. But by then thousands had been tortured on a cross—including one named Jesus Christ. Interestingly, it was out of reverence for this very Jesus that Constantine outlawed this method of execution three centuries later.

When Jesus was crucified he voluntarily took the guilt of your sins and mine to the cross with him. As death drew near, the Son of God summoned all of his human strength and said, "It is finished!"

SECOND, REALIZE THAT THERE IS A HEAVY PENALTY FOR YOUR SIN.

Except ye repent, ye shall all likewise perish. (Luke 13:3)

Wherefore, as by one man sin entered into the world, and death by sin; and so death passed upon all men, for that all have sinned. (Romans 5:12)

THIRD, ACKNOWLEDGE THAT GOD MADE A WAY FOR YOU TO BE SAVED.

For God so loved the world, that he gave his only begotten Son, that whosoever believeth in him should not perish, but have everlasting life. (John 3:16)

He humbled himself, and became obedient unto death, even the death of the cross. (Philippians 2:8)

FOURTH, ACCEPT GOD'S PLAN FOR YOUR SALVATION TODAY.

[Jesus] is able also to save them to the uttermost that come unto God by him, seeing he ever liveth to make intercession for them. (Hebrews 7:25)

But as many as received [Jesus], to them gave he power to become the sons of God, even to them that believe on his name. (John 1:12)

Read and pray the following prayer, accepting Christ personally, and God will forgive your sins and make you one of his own.

Dear Lord Jesus, I confess that I am a guilty sinner and that I need to be saved. I believe that you died on the cross to pay my sin debt. Please forgive my sins, come into my heart, and save my soul. I turn my life over to you. Help me to live for you from now on. Amen.

To read the Bible, learn about Jesus, or find a church in your area, visit **Crossway.org/LearnMore**.

CROSSWAY | GOOD NEWS Tracts

9 781682 162941

www.goodnewstracts.org

©2001 Good News Tracts. Redesign ©2016. Printed in U.S.A. Cover image: Thomas Kinkade. Bible references: KJV. Written by: Lindsay Terry.